Original title:
A Brooch's Story

Copyright © 2025 Creative Arts Management OÜ
All rights reserved.

Author: Victor Mercer
ISBN HARDBACK: 978-1-80586-041-9
ISBN PAPERBACK: 978-1-80586-513-1

Radiance of Remembrance

In a drawer of forgotten things,
A pin that dances and sweetly sings.
Once a gift from a suitor bold,
Now it sparkles with stories old.

It winks at moths with a cheeky grin,
Whispers tales of where it's been.
From evening gowns to shirts askew,
It's a shine that knows just what to do.

Timeless Trinkets

A lady wore it on her hat,
Now it plays games with the cat.
Once a chatty friend at a ball,
Now it's tangled with socks in the hall.

It teases the drawer, 'Let me out!'
Winks at the dust, ready to shout.
Each scratch and dent a story reveals,
Of simpler times and delightful deals.

OST: Objects of Stories Told

In a box marked 'Do Not Touch',
Lies a gem that won't cost much.
Once it sparkled in the bright sun,
Now it laughs, thinking of its fun.

It jingles tales like wind chimes sway,
Of fashion finds and yesterday.
With each twist, a giggle escapes,
Reminding us of all shapes and scrapes.

Relics of Romance

Once a treasure of hearts in bloom,
Now an accessory in the gloom.
It rolls its eyes at fashion snobs,
And jokes with buttons, like a mob.

In a strange world of glitter and glue,
It chuckles quietly, 'What's new?'
A relic of love, still holds its place,
Wearing time with an amusing grace.

A Dancer in the Light

She twirls and twinkles, a dazzling sight,
Caught in a shimmer, all sparkly delight.
With every twist, she bids the world cheer,
Her laughter's a melody, vibrant and clear.

A breeze pulls her gently, a playful tease,
She flutters and giggles with elegant ease.
Reflecting the frolic of life's lively flow,
In every small glimmer, it's her time to glow.

Pendant of Emotions

Hanging on laughter, she swings with a grin,
Holding all secrets, both thick and too thin.
Her heart is a whirlwind, a comedic play,
In every situation, she finds a ballet.

Oh, what a show! She juggles life's pranks,
Dancing in circles while dodging distractions and thanks.
Wearing a crown made of giggles and sighs,
A pendant of joy, oh how she just flies!

The Silent Witness

In crowded rooms, she quietly spies,
Watching the chaos with wide-open eyes.
She's heard every rumor, each whispered remark,
In her metal embrace, all secrets embark.

With every new story, she sparkles and beams,
A specter of mischief amidst laughter and dreams.
Her silence, a canvas painted with glee,
The witness to folly, hilarious and free.

Reflections in a Rhinestone

Shining in flashes, she catches a glance,
Mirroring moments, both awkward and chance.
Quirky encounters, she captures with flair,
Each spark tells a joke, in the glittering air.

With each little twinkle, a story unfolds,
Of mishaps and maybes, so charming and bold.
A playful reminder of laughter so light,
In reflections that shimmer, life's truly a delight.

Worn with Pride

On a jacket, it sparkles bright,
An eye-catching gem, oh what a sight!
Each outing, it giggles, glowing loud,
A secret symbol in the fashion crowd.

It once belonged to Grandma dear,
She wore it boldly, with a cheer.
Now I strut, feeling quite grand,
Inheritances you can understand!

Loved with Care

In a velvet box, it safely sleeps,
A nugget of joy that giggles and peeps.
Each time I wear it, I feel like a queen,
With every sparkle, a laugh can be seen.

Carefully polished, affection in store,
Worn to the party or maybe the floor.
Fingers trace stories of laughter and glee,
"Who wore it best?" - it's obviously me!

A Collector's Legacy

A cabinet filled with sparkling tales,
Each piece a memory, a laugh that prevails.
Some are quirky, and others quite bold,
In my treasure trove, such wonders unfold.

A parrot, a flower, a fish with a wink,
Each one whispers secrets, don't you think?
At gatherings, friends point, and they stare,
"Where did you find this? You go everywhere!"

The Stories Beneath the Surface

Stuck on a sweater, it's got quite a tale,
Of nights filled with laughter, we danced without fail.
It went to the beach, it swam in the sea,
Now, it rests here, a bit salty and free.

I found it with dust bunnies, lost in a drawer,
Reminded that memories are worth so much more.
With each little dent, a giggle it brings,
It's a token of joy, of wonderful things!

Echoes of the Past

In dim light, it twinkles, not far from the night,
An echo of laughter, oh what a delight!
It tells of the moments we silently shared,
Adventures to remember, and no one was scared.

With friends all around, it twirls with a breeze,
A dance of old stories that bring us to knees.
"I lost that at prom!" someone chimes with a laugh,
Worn again, it gives moments their comic epitaph.

Heirloom Heartbeats

Once perched on a great-aunt's dress,
A gem that sparked much family stress.
It claimed to cure all sorts of woes,
Yet, turned out, was just a fancy hose.

With glittering stones and tales so wild,
It once made every fashion quite reviled.
Now resting in a cabinet's dark stash,
Its stories fade like yesterday's flash.

Lost and Found in Silver

In pockets deep where treasures hide,
I found a clasp that once had pride.
It winked at me with its silver sheen,
A ghost of fashion yet unseen.

It danced on coats of long-lost years,
While causing quite a few fond jeers.
"What's this?" the folks would all inquire,
"A relic from a garage sire?"

Gemstone Reveries

A ruby winked from Grandma's chest,
Claiming to be the very best.
It sparkled, shone, and made a scene,
But was it truly what it seemed?

With every outing, a different game,
It changed its story, not quite the same.
From prince to pauper in just one night,
That gem knew how to hide its light.

Secrets Encased

Nestled in a velvet-lined tray,
A mystery I found one sunny day.
What secrets did this old pin keep?
A promise of treasures, or just a leap?

Once worn by a lady of high esteem,
Now tangled in a dusty dream.
It giggled softly with each old tale,
Of party nights that never went stale.

A Legacy in Lapis

Once a stone of ancient lore,
Worn by kings who wanted more.
Lapis blue, it sparkled bright,
Lured a thief in dead of night.

Caught him swiping, oh what luck!
Stumbled, fell—what a schlock!
Now it hangs, a tale to tell,
Of a thief that tripped and fell.

Tales of Twists and Turns

Round and round, the tales do spin,
A shiny clasp, where to begin?
It caught my eye, I took a chance,
Then danced the floor—a funny prance!

With each twist, it steered my fate,
Jumps and giggles, oh how great!
In a whirlwind, I found the truth,
A necklace once owned by a sleuth!

Shimmering Timekeeper

Once a timepiece, shimmering bright,
Ticked and tocked through day and night.
But one day, it tried to flee,
And danced away, quite carelessly!

Chasing it, I hit the door,
Did a split—what a hilarious score!
Now it sits in my old drawer,
Telling time with laughs galore!

Jewel of Nostalgia

In a box of memories, dusty and old,
A jewel of stories waiting to be told.
Once a gift from a friend so dear,
Sparkling bright like laughter's cheer.

But as I wore it to the ball,
It slipped off! Oh no, what a fall!
Now it laughs with me every night,
A shiny curse—a comical sight!

An Heirloom's Journey

Once a shiny gem of flair,
Worn by a grandma with such care.
Now it wobbles, peeks, and shakes,
Gives the cat a fright that wakes!

In the drawer, it did reside,
Tangled with dust, it tried to hide.
With a twist and turn, oh what fun,
Chasing threads 'til daylight's done!

To parties, it would love to flee,
Getting lost, absurdity!
An old mate, now with tales to spill,
Of fashion highs and roller thrills!

With a wink and a little jolt,
It's the reason for each bolt.
A laughing gem with all its might,
Thank goodness, it survived the night!

The Hidden Life of a Pin

In a box where dust bunnies play,
Lives a pin that's bright and gay.
Winks at the socks it once adorned,
Now it schemes with yarns well-worn.

Forgotten tales of party dread,
Stuck in blouses, often misled.
Each poke was a stitching blunder,
Yet made a fashion statement under!

When pulled from slumber, it's quite a sight,
Ready to dance, to spark delight!
With every twist, it starts to grin,
In its heart, a golden kin.

It dreams of days both bright and loud,
Amongst the fancy, it feels proud.
Oh, the mischief it could declare,
If only it had a plush velvet chair!

Bonded by Beauty

Two pins once met on a fancy dress,
Complimenting each other's finesse.
With glimmering jokes and playful jibes,
They spun a tale of golden vibes.

In competition, they'd often prance,
Creating chaos on the dance floor, a romance!
They'd attach to outfits in a snappy way,
Ensuring all styles would win the day.

Faced with the danger of a washer's whirl,
They held on tight, giving the spin a twirl.
Who knew such pins could form a bond,
In tangled threads, beyond and beyond!

Now they rest in a drawer of dreams,
Retelling tales of glittering themes.
As friends forever, they toast and cheer,
To life's wild fabric, with charm sincere!

The Collector's Memory

A collector walked with eager hands,
Gathering treasures from distant lands.
"Oh, this gem!" they'd squeal with glee,
Each piece a laugh, a memory!

One pin, a rogue, looks out with flair,
Sporting stories of mishap and wear.
Stuck on sweaters and careless seams,
In the end, it still fulfills dreams.

Each item whispers, "Take me home!"
From park picnics to the beach foam.
They know that style can't be boxed tight,
And bold is the heart that sparkles bright!

In a glass case, each piece takes a stand,
Tales of laughter, perfectly planned.
For a collector's heart is never dull,
It's the quirkiest art that makes them full!

Whispers of Adornment

On the jacket sits a gem,
Like a laughter caught in time,
It twinkles at the dinner's whim,
A sassy chat, a fashion crime.

Once lost in the couch's fold,
It found a fortune, or so it claimed,
With crumbs beneath the gleaming gold,
Our fashion sense—forever shamed!

A cat pawed at its shiny face,
Then thought better of the chase,
In sparkly peace, it took its place,
Where no one dares to outpace.

Each pin and clasp has tales to tell,
Of awkward dances, slips, and falls,
Yet here it sits, so bright and swell,
The beacon of the laughered halls.

Memories Worn Close

A flash of color on a scarf,
It winks as if it knows,
The clumsy date, the silly laugh,
And all the joy that overflows.

Once it dressed a koala bear,
Now it's stuck on Auntie May,
With tales of parties, wild and rare,
Of fashion wins, and dreadful fray.

The pin's a cousin to the fun,
When folks forget their sense of style,
It whispers, play! Let's run! Let's run!
In sparkly chaos, that's our smile.

Tales of a tie that had to bend,
Of brave adventures, skirmishes won,
With memories stitched, time won't end,
As long as we all laugh and run.

The Pin That Tells

A little pin, a tiny muse,
It nudges me, let's make a fuss,
With every jab, it shares the news,
Of fashion wins and joyous thruss.

Stuck upon a shirt so bright,
It giggles when I trip and stumble,
In every glance, it holds me tight,
Awkward charm, it makes me grumble.

At parties, it directs the scene,
A dance, a fall, a swirl of light,
The talk of beads, so crisp and clean,
Yet here I am, a hapless sight.

With secrets held in every clasp,
The little pin, my fashion kin,
Together we will seize, and clasp,
Laughing through thick and thin.

Spark of Elegance

A sparkly bling gives quite the tease,
It jabs me when I look away,
"Oh darling, don't you feel at ease?
With me, you'll shine, come what may!"

It dances on my lapel with flair,
Challenging all that walk this lane,
With laughter bright and silly air,
To make me smile in some disdain.

Once held hostage in a drawer,
It fought my socks with grit and grace,
Now struggles for attention more,
With each bright blend, it finds its place.

So here we are, just full of glee,
Adventures, jokes, and echoing fun,
In every shine, a sight to see,
Forever playful, everyone!

Through the Ages in Gold

Once on a lady's coat it did shine,
Sparkling so bright, it thought it divine.
"Look at me!" it gleefully yelled,
As it clung to her lapel, it felt compelled.

But then came a gust, a blustery blow,
Off flew the brooch like a crow on the go!
It tumbled and rolled, causing quite a scene,
"Can I get back?" it begged, feeling quite mean.

Years went by, covered in dust,
Fallen in laughter, the world full of rust.
Yet still it would dream of a time so bold,
When it dazzled the heart—oh, the ages in gold!

Now in a drawer, it waits for a chance,
To sparkle again and invite to a dance.
With tales of the past still twinkling in eyes,
It caresses the fabric, longing for skies.

The Charm of the Unseen

In a dim drawer, so tucked away,
Lies a tiny gem with much to say.
It whispers of days full of laughter and joy,
Of crisp autumn leaves and a mischievous toy.

It once had a home on a bright yellow dress,
Commanding the room, oh, what a finesse!
"Flaunt me!" it laughed, on a date with a crown,
But the lady forgot, and it tumbled down.

Now it tells stories to dust bunnies near,
Of times when it sparkled, full of good cheer.
"Oh, the charm of the unseen," it worthily beams,
"Rescue me quick! Let's fulfill our dreams!"

In hopes of a moment, it twinkles with zeal,
To sit once again, an elegant spiel.
Who knows what it'll find, with a slight nudge and squeak?
Perhaps it's the magic of hide-and-seek!

An Ornament's Odyssey

Once on an expedition, an ornament bold,
Sailed through the night, with stories untold.
It whispered to stars, to the moon's gentle light,
"Watch out world! I'm a serious sight!"

But alas, poor gem, it lost all its flair,
As it rolled off a table, with a shuddering scare!
Crashing to ground, oh what a disgrace,
It lay there in silence, missing the chase.

Through bustling bazaars and glitzy boutiques,
It was left behind, oh the irony peaks.
It yearned for a body, a show of applause,
As it fidgeted there, in dust and in gauze.

But fret not, dear brooch, for tales yet to spin,
A shine will return, when the right mood begins.
Adventures await, so let out a cheer,
The odyssey of life is more fun with a smear!

Layers of Affection

In a pile of sweaters, it lay with disdain,
A gem full of hopes, feeling quite plain.
"I once was the star!" it cried with delight,
"Clinging to silk, oh, what a sweet flight!"

Yet time marches on, and so do the trends,
Now it's a throwback; nostalgia bends.
"Why was I shelved?" it pondered with mirth,
"I'm layered in laughter, despite my dearth!"

Each season brings change, like a tick-tock of fate,
Dressed up for parties, or hiding till late.
It chuckled through years, though squished with the folds,
For friendship nurtures, and affection unfolds.

So here's to the moments, both grand and serene,
To layers of love that quilt our routine.
It may seem quite silly, but in the right light,
The laughs of a gem can spark endless delight!

Forgotten Secrets of Wear

Once nestled shyly on a lapel,
Caught in a dance of dust and spell,
Faded colors, secrets to share,
Awakening giggles from wear and tear.

A witty wink from old attire,
Whispers of laughter, sparking a fire,
What tales weaved in silken threads,
Of flirty nights and fancy spreads.

Stuck in a drawer, longing for the light,
To reunite with clothes that feel just right,
Oh, how it chuckles, our peppy friend,
That glinting treasure, time cannot bend.

Through decades past, a quirky charm,
Pinning mishaps, a fashionable harm,
With every poke, it teases the past,
A escapade of style, forever to last.

Echoes of a Gilded Past

This trinket recalls a lavish soirée,
Where laughter echoed and worries drifted away,
A twist and a turn in the brightest light,
Tales of a dance, oh what a sight!

Hitching a ride on a flamboyant dress,
It's been a witness to fun and finesse,
With memories sparkling, it chuckles so bold,
It's a jester of shadows, continuing to hold.

Once the centerpiece of a party's delight,
Glimpses of joy in the deep of the night,
Retelling stories with a wink and a gleam,
This silly adornment lives for the dream.

It sat on a shelf, dormant and shy,
Until one day, a bold lady passed by,
With a snap and a smile, it found its new place,
Igniting the laughter, with exclamations of grace.

The Keeper's Touch

A flamboyant clasp, so proud and bright,
It dances on fabric with sheer delight,
The keeper's touch, both witty and grand,
Spinning tales across the land.

In an attic so dusty, it played peek-a-boo,
With memories stuck like an old shoe,
Histories tangled in sparkling embrace,
Oh, the mischief it's seen in its space!

Oh! To catch a glimpse of fashion's time,
This playful pin crafts an elaborate rhyme,
Every whirl brings chuckles and cheer,
As clothes take a spin, 'round again, here!

It wonders if it's a unique delight,
A fashionista's favorite or just polite,
With every sparkle, it plays a new part,
A giggling gem, and a painter of art.

Charmed Encounters

On a bustling street, it met quite the eye,
With a twinkle and flutter, it breathed a sigh,
A serendipitous clash of fate with a grin,
A charming encounter, let the fun begin!

Tickling the neck of a fancy blouse,
This character winks, oh so douse,
With stories to tell through threads sublime,
Secret rendezvous of laughter and rhyme.

At fancy balls or quiet retreats,
It tickles the fabric where laughter meets,
Sharing the glow of a silver moon,
With an infectious chuckle, humming a tune.

Each glance is a giggle, a merry delight,
This ornament's heart always feels light,
Charmed encounters that never grow old,
In fashion's embrace, memories unfold.

Muted Whispers of Beauty

In a drawer, a trinket lies,
A shiny gem with sparkly eyes.
Once it danced with joyful flair,
Now it waits, a tale to share.

It once adorned a lovely dress,
But now it's just a dusty mess.
A fateful toss, a drunken night,
Left it hanging, oh what a sight!

Its stories hum a silent song,
Of times when it felt bold and strong.
A party here, a wedding there,
Now it's stuck in timeless glare.

Yet still it gleams with silly pride,
A tiny gem with nowhere to hide.
One day it'll sparkle, oh so bright,
Till then, it's just a laugh at night.

A Tangle of Memories

Oh, how it twirls through memory seams,
A charming clip with outlandish dreams.
Once pinned on hats, now in the ditch,
A fashionista's forgotten witch.

Once it held a flower's grace,
Now it's dusting off its face.
With every twist, a giggle's found,
In every pin, a story bound.

Yet still it smiles with winks and sighs,
Recalling days when it was wise.
It once made people laugh and cheer,
Now just nudges from the rear.

Perhaps one day, it'll take a ride,
On a thrill-seeker's flashy side.
But for now, it sits in glee,
With memories of a fashion spree.

Ephemeral Elegance

Shimmery sparkles on a coat,
Once a star, now barely afloat.
With frolic dreams, it took its flight,
Now just a laugh in the moonlight.

It caught the eye at every event,
But now its glory feels quite spent.
The night it slipped, oh what a fall,
From grandeur to a silly brawl.

Yet in those shines of time, it beams,
Reminding us of once bright dreams.
An elegant jest in drab disguise,
Whispering tales with twinkling eyes.

It waits for style to come around,
To laugh again with joy unbound.
For elegance, though it may wane,
Can always find a way to reign.

The Fabric of Sentiment

In a world of style, it made its mark,
A quirky piece, a little spark.
Sewn with tales of laughter and tears,
Now a relic of forgotten years.

Once admired on a velvet facade,
It's tangled in memories, oh so odd.
From frothy parties to baking fails,
It winks at mishaps, a tale that sails.

"Remember when?" the stories start,
Of slips and trips that love impart.
Amidst the clutter, it finds its tune,
Weaving joy like a bright balloon.

It may fade in the fashion spree,
But in our hearts, it'll always be.
A laugh, a smile, a silly glance,
In the fabric of life's wild dance.

A Pin's Perspective

In a drawer so snug and tight,
I dream of shiny days and night.
With fabric friends, I like to play,
but I always stab them in the fray.

Satin whispers, oh so sleek,
I poke and prod, oh what a freak!
My pointy dance, it makes folks laugh,
while I just roll, 'What a gaffe!'

Bobbins giggle, threads entwine,
and I just scheme, 'This thread is mine!'
A safety pin just rolls its eyes,
while I flaunt my daring ties.

So here's my tale, quite absurd and light,
I reign supreme in fabric fights.
Who needs a crown or fancy thing?
When you're a pin, you're always king!

Tales from the Pin Cushion

Nestled here amongst my kin,
I've tales of thread, let the fun begin!
With every poke, a giggle bursts,
who knew this cushion had such quirks?

Buttons bounce and zippers snort,
while needles hold a snipping court.
In patchwork land, I find my place,
as I embrace this needle race.

A thimble sings a tune or two,
and tells of fabric that just wouldn't do.
With every prick, a story told,
in this little world, we break the mold.

So gather 'round and lend an ear,
as needles laugh and threads draw near.
In this cotton kingdom, we will stay,
stitching up the fun, come what may!

The Twinkle of Forgotten Days

Once a shiny clasp on a dress,
now a closet's quiet mess.
Oh, the parties lost in time,
where I sparkled, oh so prime!

Dust bunnies roll, they know the score,
while I yearn for the dance floor.
I whisper tales of nights so grand,
when I sparkled, held by a hand.

But now I'm stuck with socks and shoes,
adorned by lint, what a ruse!
Yet every time the sun's rays peek,
I remember nights of laughter's cheek.

So here I lie with stories old,
of laughter shared, of glitz and gold.
I may be hiding from the light,
but oh, those days were pure delight!

Shimmering Shadows

In a dusty box, I catch the light,
shimmering shadows, a marvelous sight.
I once adorned the finest dress,
but now I lie, oh what a mess!

Derby hats and gloves all tease,
while I'm just here, collecting breeze.
Oh, the parties where I reigned,
now all my glimmer feels so contained.

Once a crown on a casual night,
now I dwell in a forgotten plight.
Yet sometimes a flicker brings me cheer,
with memories, oh so dear!

So let me sparkle, though days have passed,
because humor's light, it forever lasts.
In my little box, I sparkle still,
waiting for the day, a chance to thrill!

The Forgotten Embrace

In a drawer lost and confined,
A shiny pin waits, unaligned.
It dreams of a blouse, bright and bold,
But dust bunnies dance, and it's left out in the cold.

Once adored, with a twinkle and flair,
It sparkled on jackets, with style to spare.
Now it munches on crumbs, a snack for the mice,
Thinking of parties, oh, once it was nice!

It sighs to the ribboned, the laces nearby,
"Oh, how I've missed glimmering high!"
The other old trinkets just roll their eyes,
"Dream on, dear pin, you're not a surprise!"

But in dreams it's a star, taking center stage,
With laughter and fun, oh, the tales it could sage.
One day it might shine, in a fashion parade,
For now, it will rest, a forgotten charade.

A Pinch of History

In ancient times, a mighty flair,
A little pin with tales to share.
It glued rivals on the floor,
In jest, they'd trip, oh, what's in store!

Worn by queens and jester's hat,
It sparkled while they laughed and spat.
A history of giggles, quiet sneers,
This tiny tale has survived the years.

Now resting in a chest, quite chic,
Awaiting fashion's next little tweak.
It giggles at stories, none like the last,
Pinching humor from days long past.

With whispers of ruffles and fabric bends,
It recalls the mischief and silly trends.
"Oh, to be worn," it sighs in delight,
For once again, it could shine through the night.

Fashioned Fantasies

In a box of wonders, there lies a scheme,
A pin with dreams, like a fairy tale theme.
It wishes for gowns, ballrooms to grace,
But here with the buttons, it's lost all its space.

It's seen the world through a velvet glance,
Imagining glamour in a grand dance.
Yet here it remains, in clutter and fluff,
Pining for moments of sparkle and puff.

"Oh dear little clown, don't wear me with fright,
I could make you dazzling, like a star in the night!"
Yet every time it gets picked up with dread,
The wearer just fumbles, then shakes their head.

Yet still, it dreams of a whimsical fate,
Of laughter and fashion, it joyfully waits.
Someday it will dazzle, in comical style,
For now, it just grins, and hangs out for a while.

A Kiss of Glamour

Oh, what a prize with a shimmer and wink,
A tiny embellishment, that's made us all think.
A dash of brilliance on a garment plain,
It's the life of the party, it craves for the gain.

In the realm of fabric where styles collide,
It sprinkles some laughs, spreading joy wide.
A little wild, with a flair for the fun,
When pinned on the collar, it leaves everyone stunned.

Dancing through closets, it's mastered the art,
Of turning a dull piece into a heart.
With stories of mischief, it lends to each wear,
It knows it's the star, with laughter to spare.

And as it glimmers, bright as a smile,
Showing off elegance with a touch of style.
It's not just a trinket, but friendships it brings,
A kiss of glamour, oh, how it sings!

A Metal's Medley

In a drawer filled with treasures, they play,
A silver spoon jokes with a rusty nail.
"Look at my shine!" cries a flashy pin,
While the old key chuckles, "You'll never win!"

A gold ring laughs, spinning tales of old,
"I'm the star of the box, bright and bold."
But the paper clip winks, sly and shrewd,
"I hold it together, while you're just crude!"

The thimble does tumbles, so clumsy and round,
"In a world of fine jewels, I'm rarely found!"
Yet they all dance together, quite merry and loud,
In the quirky little box, they're a cheerful crowd!

So here's to the metals, each with their charm,
In the drawer of laughter, they weave a warm balm.
Let them sparkle and jest, with stories anew,
For who knew that those little trinkets could do?

The Light in the Dark

In shadows they linger, a glimmer unfolds,
A shiny old pin with tales to be told.
"I once sparked a dance at a grand masquerade,
Now I'm here snoozing, my glory just fade!"

A tiny old charm chimes in with a grin,
"I've seen all your antics, now let's let the fun begin!"
As the night wears on, they giggle and dream,
In the corners of darkness, they twinkle and beam.

A chunky old buckle laughs, full of pride,
"I keep all the pants, you can't push me aside!"
Yet they all know the truth, it's the laughter that shines,
In the box of forgotten, where humor entwines!

So hold tight to the dark, where the silly ones play,
For light comes from laughter, at the end of the day.
Each twist, each turn, a delightful surprise,
In this whimsical tale, joy always will rise!

Sparkling Chronicles

Once an earring, lost but never alone,
Rode the waves of laughter, in a sea of chrome.
"I've swayed to the music, danced with such flair,
Now I'm clipped to a hat, but hey, life's not fair!"

A locket with secrets, whispering dreams,
"Remember the kisses?" it beams and it beams.
"Oh, the love that I held, wrapped close to the heart,
Now I'm a paperweight, but still, I'm a part!"

A pin with a sparkle boasts stories of grace,
"I've graced countless dresses, what a lovely place!"
But the hairpin rolls eyes, with a flick of its head,
"You glitter and shine, but dear, I hold the thread!"

In the chronicles of metal, each has its role,
From wear, to the wall, to the secretive soul.
So let's raise a toast to all that you see,
For every little trinket holds humor with glee!

A Legacy of Shine

In a box full of wonders, ancestral few,
Shimmering legacy, with stories so true.
"I'm a badge of honor, once worn with great pride,
Now I'm a relic, hiding in the tide!"

A pair of lost cufflinks chat with a grin,
"Remember the parties? Let the fun begin!"
With tales of old dances and drinks raised so high,
Together they sparkle, under the same sky.

A compass with direction points far and wide,
"Once I led adventures, now to the side!"
Yet every glimmer still holds its own fate,
In the laughter of metals, they merrily wait!

So here's to the legacy, bright and absurd,
Each tale holds a chuckle, a melody heard.
Let them twinkle and shine in their whimsical dance,
For life's a grand party, give metal a chance!

Sentiments in Silver

On a coat so grand, I took my seat,
But then I fell, oh what a feat!
The pin was sly, it made me fumble,
Lost my dignity, but what a jumble.

A party of bright, sparkly sights,
Caught in a chat, as day turns to nights.
Adorned with glee, I stood so proud,
Till someone asked, "Is that your crowd?"

In mirrors reflecting, I shine and gleam,
But watch out, my friend, it's not as it seems.
I winked at the people, my charm so bold,
Yet tales of mishaps were quickly retold.

From clasping hearts to a fashion faux pas,
Silver holds secrets under the stars.
With laughter resounding, we dance and tease,
This little tale, it never brings grief.

The Art of Attachment

On a blouse, I felt oh so grand,
But alas, was left without a hand.
My partner in crime was stuck in place,
As I twirled about in that lively space.

"I'll hold you tight!" my owner declared,
But with one sharp move, we both were scared.
The latch released—what a sight to behold,
Flying through air, like a story told.

Clipping and clopping, I danced on air,
Dodging a drink, oh do take care!
Now I'm a legend, a star on the scene,
With tales of mischief, oh, how I've been!

From sidekick to star, in every attire,
The art of attachment, what a wild fire!
With laughter and flair, we'll take on the night,
Together we sparkle, oh what a delight!

Stories Embedded in Gold

Once on a lapel, I had my day,
A royal affair, I stole the display.
But a gust of wind, oh what a folly,
I flipped and flopped, my moment quite jolly.

"I'm the next big trend," I proudly recited,
Yet off I went, the crowd so excited.
Chasing my dreams down a fancy lane,
With giggles and snickers, I felt no shame.

In gleaming glory, I sailed in style,
Tickling whiskers of folks with a smile.
"Oh dear!" they laughed, as I twinkled bright,
A story of laughter, through day and night.

From whispers of gold, to stories of cheer,
I gather the moments that we hold dear.
With each silly twist, and every big fold,
A gold-plated journey, forever retold!

Radiance of Recollections

Nestled in a box, I waited my turn,
For laughter and joy was what I did yearn.
When a dress called to me, so vivid, so bright,
I knew I was ready to take to flight.

"Oh my," said she, "What a lovely piece!"
But in my excitement, I caused a caprice.
The clasp went awry, I flew through the air,
Creating a spectacle, causing a scare.

Lines of wide laughter surrounded my grace,
I sparkled and glinted, a comical race.
With memories stitched in each shimmer and glow,
I turned frowns upside down; I stole the show!

So gather 'round close, as tales intertwine,
In moments of humor, our hearts all align.
For each splash of color, every giggle bestowed,
Is a radiant treasure, a story well-sowed.

The Charm of Time

On a shirt, so shiny and bright,
A tiny pin sparkles with delight.
Once a gift from a grandma dear,
Now it dances, spreading cheer.

In the drawer, it likes to hide,
Claiming it's on a fashion ride.
It twirls and laughs, oh what a game,
Making all the buttons feel lame.

At parties, it steals the show,
Winking to friends, in a lively flow.
"I'm the best accessory here,"
It whispers sweetly, loud and clear.

So if you see this twinkling pin,
Remember, it's where the fun begins.
Time may pass, but it won't grow old,
With stories of laughter yet untold.

Jewelry's Pathway

Down the aisle, it rolls away,
Chasing light like it's a game to play.
With a flick and a twist, it leaps,
Telling tales of secrets it keeps.

From hand to hand, it finds its way,
A dance of gems, come what may.
It whispers jokes to every ring,
In a world where they all sing.

Through the years, it's made quite a mess,
Tangled with ribbons, I must confess.
It giggles at mirrors, striking poses,
Making friends with curious roses.

So next time you see it strut,
Remember the mischief, oh what a rut!
Jewelry's path is full of cheer,
With every twist, magic is near.

Time's Little Treasures

In a corner, it lies with pride,
Tales of adventures it cannot hide.
Once a pirate's eye-catching tool,
Now a legend that breaks every rule.

It's wobbly and weird, but we all agree,
No other pin can match this glee.
With charms that rattle, and colors so bright,
It spins around, ready for flight.

When kids come by to give it a peek,
It shows off its flair, oh so unique.
Together they giggle, they share their dreams,
The pin's clever antics fill up the seams.

Zipping and zapping, it takes a bow,
With laughter that bubbles, it steals the show.
Time's little treasures, they gleam and sway,
In a funny dance that won't fade away.

Tales of a Glittering Past

Resting on velvet, it tells a tale,
Of parties and laughter, it hails.
Once a star on a frock, newly wed,
Now it just laughs at the cat instead.

In dusty corners, it thrives on gossip,
Of quarrels and marriages, it won't stop.
Who knew a little pin could jest,
With history tucked in its shiny chest?

With a wink it says, "Take me for tea!"
"I'll spice up your outfit, just wait and see."
It giggles with beads, as it clinks and clinks,
Reminiscing of all those fun little kinks.

Oh, the stories it holds, wrapped in gold,
Of fates intertwined and laughter bold.
Tales of a glittering past will forever dance,
In the hearts of those who dare to prance.

Chronicles of a Dazzling Past

Once I sparkled on a dress,
A giggle here, a silly mess.
Held tight through laughter, dance, and cheer,
Now I'm lost, but don't shed a tear.

From fancy parties to the cat's play,
I rolled around in a clumsy sway.
Forgotten in a drawer so deep,
Now I plot my grand escape!

Every twist of thread and clasp,
I feel the weight of memories grasp.
A life of charm, now tucked away,
I long for nights of bright cabaret.

So here I wait, a gem unseen,
Waiting for a time machine.
To dance once more with flair and zest,
And find a place where I am blessed.

The Allure of the Lost

Oh how I twinkled in the light,
Adorned a collar, oh so bright.
Left behind at a summer's race,
Now I'm stuck in this lonely place.

I hear the tales of nights long gone,
Of laughter shared till the dawn.
A penguin costume and a spilled drink,
The memories make me smile and wink.

In a purse with crumbs and receipts,
I wonder of my former feats.
Oh, the stories I could still tell,
With charm and humor, oh so well!

If only hands could dig me out,
I'd charm again, there's little doubt.
A shiny beacon of joy once more,
I'd dance and sparkle, shake the floor.

Enchanted Keepsake

Nestled tight in a velvet pouch,
I felt quite grand, not a bit slouch.
From royal balls to grandma's tea,
I've had my share of jubilee!

I graced the neck of a fairy queen,
Who tripped on air and lost her sheen.
I giggled hard when she fell down,
The sparkling gem became a clown!

Then one wild night, amidst the fun,
I rolled away, my races begun.
Through alleyways of gossip and cheer,
I hid from all, but none drew near.

So here I lie with tales to tell,
In the hopes of fame, I'll ring the bell.
To shine once more and spill my tales,
Of goofy dances, laughter, and trails.

Unspoken Affinities

I once had a buddy, a flashy hat,
Together we roamed, imagine that!
We'd strut in style through a crowded street,
But he vanished quick, oh such a feat!

I hopped on suits, I twinkled proud,
At every party, I rocked the crowd.
But having lost my dear little mate,
Danced alone and pondered fate.

With each clink of glass, I missed our laughs,
He was the zinger; I was the sass!
Now I sit, a lone little gem,
Hoping for a partner from a distant realm.

But don't you fret, dear onlookers dear,
For each lost friend comes with a cheer.
The friendship sparkles eternal and bright,
In my shiny world, we reunite!

Elegance Worn

On a jacket, it sits so proud,
A shiny gem, drawing a crowd.
A butterfly in a field of gray,
It flaps its wings and steals the day.

Once a gift from Grandma dear,
Now a staple, let's make it clear.
It's seen some parties, oh what fun,
But fell in soup—oops! Now it's done.

Dancing on my collarbone,
It wobbles like it's on its own.
Held by a pin, a brave little stunt,
Fashion's friend or a food hunt?

With every twist, it tells a tale,
Of daring looks and wardrobe fail.
In the closet, it hopes to shine,
A little sparkle, always divine!

Through the Gaze of Glamour

Once a trinket in a dusty box,
Now it struts like a peacock, it rocks!
With a wink, it catches the light,
Who knew such joy could bring delight?

Adorned on a hat that's far too big,
It sways and dances, just like a jig.
Sparkling with mischief at every turn,
If hats could talk, oh what they'd learn!

Can it outshine a diamond bright?
In my dreams, it claims that right.
But wait—what's that? It fell in the stew!
A shimmering splash? Oh, who knew?

It giggles and glimmers, what a show,
A wardrobe hero, with flair in tow.
Through laughter and joy, it steals the stage,
In the theater of life, it's all the rage!

The Adorned Journey

From grandma's box, it began its quest,
A sparkle here, a twinkle, the best.
To fairs and markets, it hitched a ride,
Though a few times, it's nearly died!

Once on a coat, it felt quite grand,
But slipped in the mud—oh, how it planned!
With a splash and a laugh, it came back clean,
A mud-mixed gem, still bright and keen.

Next, on a bag that's seen better days,
It turned heads in the funniest ways.
A lady looked and let out a giggle,
"Oh dear, did it just do a wiggle?"

Now a tale that's endless and sweet,
It brings joy wherever it will meet.
With charm and laughter, it spins a yarn,
An adventure worn with a touch of charm!

Heartfelt With Glimmer

Once a gift, but what a find!
In a drawer, it stayed entwined.
With a pop and a flare, it took a leap,
Now it sparkles, and no one can sleep.

Fastened to coats or holding a scarf,
It flirts and twirls, oh what a laugh!
It shines with such glee, a playful spark,
No night too dark, it leaves its mark.

In bakery corners, near pastries and pies,
A sprinkle of flour has seen its highs.
"Oh no!" cries the baker, laughing delight,
"Your glimmer's too bright; don't take a bite!"

With each little giggle, it holds our hearts,
A charming gem with its many parts.
In a world of gray, it brings the day,
A glimmering laugh on the fun-filled way!

The Glimmering Thread

In a drawer of oddities it lays,
Spinning yarns of olden days.
Each sparkle carries a silly grin,
Whispers of moments buried within.

A dance with a button, a fight with a pin,
Master of mischief, where to begin?
Once stole the show at a wedding so grand,
The bride thought it more than just planned!

With threads of gold and stories so bright,
It twinkles and winks in the fading light.
Each twist and turn, a laugh to unfold,
A tale of wonder worth more than gold.

So here it remains, a jester on chest,
A treasure that gleams, never at rest.
Bound to the laughter that lingers near,
A glimmering thread, forever a cheer.

Echoes on a Chain

Once lost in a pond, now swinging around,
Echoes of laughter in every sound.
Hitchhiked on a blouse, what a bold ride,
Each jingle a giggle, nowhere to hide.

Chased by a cat, slipped under a chair,
Part of the gag, but who really cares?
A wisecrack of color, all clashing delight,
Makes every dull outfit instantly bright.

In the closet, a secret, its hidden domain,
Lives in the shadows, oh what a campaign!
Waiting for mischief, a chance to be seen,
An echoing laughter in whimsical sheen.

So when you wear it, just know it will play,
Telling funny tales in its own quirky way.
Each link like a laugh, a circle of fun,
In retrospect, maybe it's second to none.

Trinkets and Tales

A trinket with tales, so charming, so sly,
It tells of adventures in every nearby.
Adrift on a scarf, it waves with delight,
Daring the moon to join in the night.

Each little story, a minuscule stunt,
A misadventure, a grand little hunt.
It led a parade of lost socks through time,
On a quest for the perfect rhyme!

What's this? A car chase? A tussle with fate?
A sprint at the mall—it really was great!
A witness to giggles, and friendship's embrace,
With a wink, it joins in the fun-loving race.

So come listen close, to its whimsical sound,
For trinkets like these are quite rarely found.
To wear is to share in a grand merry tale,
Oh, the joy of a trinket that never goes stale.

Worn Stories

Once vibrant and bold, now slightly askew,
Worn stories unfold just for you.
Nestled in fabric, beside a small seam,
Lives a life filled with giggles and dreams.

From formal affairs to a night in the park,
This gem had its moments, a bright little spark.
With mischief and charm, it caught every glance,
Surprising the crowd with a comical dance.

It's seen spilled drinks and shoes made for prance,
Holding together a fashion's last chance.
Each dent and each scratch tells a laughable tale,
A patchwork of memories, never to pale.

So wear it with pride, let its stories unfold,
A stitch in your life, with laughter to hold.
For pieces like this, with heart and with glee,
Are truly the treasures that let us be free.

Reflections in a Gem

Once upon a shiny day,
A gem took to the streets to play.
It sparkled in the sun so bright,
Waving hello with pure delight.

It met a button, quite a clown,
Who told it jokes that wore a frown.
They laughed until they both turned red,
And hatched a plan to dance instead.

But when they twirled, a thread came loose,
The button frowned, feeling the noose.
The gem just giggled, said, "Don't pout,
Let's shine together, there's no doubt!"

At night, they twinkled in the moon,
A duo drawing quite a tune.
They danced on ceilings, made folks gawk,
A gem and button, what a talk!

Sentiments Encapsulated

Nestled in a velvet case,
Lies a relic of funny grace.
Two hearts entwined with a silly bow,
Whispering secrets from long ago.

A lady wore it during tea,
Made friends laugh so joyfully.
It winked at prude from across the room,
Causing giggles to swiftly bloom.

Once it was lost beneath a chair,
The gossip it heard? Beyond compare!
It learned of love, and tales of woe,
While trapped in dust, too shy to show.

When finally found, it sparked good cheer,
With stories that would bring a tear.
Now it shines, as laughter flows,
A trinket of joy that forever glows.

The Legacy of Sparkle

In a drawer full of forgotten dreams,
A shiny relic plots its schemes.
It wishes to dance, it wishes to shine,
To pop up in outfits that are divine!

It once adorned a grand affair,
Which ended in confetti and a wild hair.
The wearer tripped on her own two feet,
That brooch bounced, oh, what a feat!

Now it lies there, dreaming bold,
Of glitzy nights and moments untold.
A legacy of sparkle, a life of sass,
It's waiting for chance to kick some… class!

So take it out, give it a whirl,
Time to let it shine and twirl!
For every gem has laughter's tone,
With stories that are all its own.

A Pin's Portrait

On a canvas made of silk and thread,
Lies a pin with ideas in its head.
It sketches dreams in tiny strokes,
Reviving memories, giggles, and jokes.

At costume parties, it steals the show,
With stories that only it can know.
It's traveled far, and it's seen it all,
From grand galas to the silliest ball.

With every twinkle lights a spark,
It whispers tales from dawn till dark.
It once graced a jester's flashy attire,
Making everyone's laughter reach higher.

So lift this pin, and spin its yarn,
For every tale brings a new charm.
In fun and laughter, it finds its place,
A portrait of joy wrapped in grace.

Lace of Time

Once I was a simple thread,
Caught in a seam, living in dread.
But then a lady found me bright,
Stitched me on, brought me to light.

Dancing around in glamorous flair,
I overheard gossips beyond compare.
Tickled by tales of how I shine,
Every clasp, a sip of fine wine.

Oh, the stories that I could tell,
Of all the places where I've dwelled.
From a hat to a scarf, even a shoe,
Who knew my life would be so askew?

Now I sit proudly on her dress,
Feeling like royalty, feeling blessed.
A simple twist, a grander plot,
Who knew an accessory makes a hotspot?

Dazzle of Sentience

In a box of trinkets, I was found,
Awake in a dream, twirling around.
Sparkling with laughter, I had to chime,
A dance of joy, oh what a time!

I heard the whispers of cloth and thread,
Stories like popcorn—bubbly, widespread.
In my shiny world, everyone's a clown,
With every pin, I'd turn the frown.

Once a pendant swore it was a star,
I told him, buddy, you're not that far!
In this gathering of glitz and Giggle,
Even the dullest can make us wiggle.

At parties, my shine brings out the jest,
With every wear, I'm a guest of honor, no less.
I may be small, but I hold such glee,
In this crazy world, I'm the VIP!

Threads of Yesterday

In the attic, I was tucked away,
Stories of old, mapping the way.
Touched by fingers, as time went by,
I murmured secrets, a heartfelt sigh.

With each glance, a tale unfolds,
Of dances, laughter, and loves retold.
Once a wild child, now I stay mute,
Yet my glimmering heart will always salute.

A button once dragged me out to play,
We twirled and skipped, hip-hip-hooray!
Through breezy winters and summer's heat,
I laughed with life, oh what a treat!

But now I rest, as days go by,
A cherished rumble in the memory sky.
Tales woven softly, heartstrings they pull,
Even in quiet, I'm never quite full.

Heartbeats in Gemstone

I was once a rough little stone,
Hidden away, feeling all alone.
But then they polished me, gave me flair,
Now I strut like I'm the fairest of fair.

With every twist, I catch the eye,
Like a peacock, I spread, oh my!
A fitting here, a clasp over there,
I'm a superstar, without a care!

In a jewelry box, full of clinks,
Blinging around, we all share winks.
Gems exchange tales of love and wars,
Feelings that sparkle behind closed doors.

From necklaces to tiaras, I roam free,
In the realm of glam, I'm meant to be.
A tiny heart beating amidst the shine,
With laughter and joy, I call it divine!

www.ingramcontent.com/pod-product-compliance
Lightning Source LLC
Chambersburg PA
CBHW060143230426
43661CB00003B/543